How to Know the Will of God for Your Life

God has a Plan
And Your Life has a Purpose

David Holdaway

Copyright © David Holdaway 2017

E-mail: davidholdaway1@aol.com

www.lifepublications.org.uk

Cover design by Graeme Moodie
ISBN 9781907929786

Dedication

To an amazing group of men and women on fire for God and with a passion to know and do His will

The Bible College of Wales Autumn Class of 2016

Amanda Koh
Amy Lim Seok Wei
Audris Quek
Bethany Thompson
Carol Yeo
Carrie Warren
Christine Roles
Dennis Boon
Eryn Cummings
Ettienne Hand
Fabian Tang
Faye Shen
Jeremiah Chor
Jeremy Chew
Jimson Cheng
Linda Saville
Lisa Lim
Mae Jover
Maggie Tan
Matthew Sims
Michelle Woo
Natalia Fuentes
Nicole Pearce
Nidia Meneses
Priscilla Chua
Rachel Yong
Sam Ong
Sandra Wade
Seok Lim
Serene Seow
Solomon Hng
Suzanne Soh
Maria Marciano
Yao Yi Koh

How to Know the Will of God

The Will of God

The will of God will never take you
Where the grace of God cannot keep you,
Where the arms of God cannot support you,
Where the provision of God cannot supply you.

The will of God will never take you
Where the power of God cannot enable you,
Where the Spirit of God cannot work through you,
Where the resources of God cannot equip you.

The will of God will never take you
Where the hand of God cannot protect you,
Where the love of God cannot enfold you,
Where the peace of God cannot sustain you.

The will of God will never take you
Where the goodness of God cannot follow you,
Where the mercy of God cannot reach you,
Where the joy of the Lord cannot strengthen you.

The will of God will never take you
Where the wisdom of God cannot instruct you,
Where the comfort of God cannot embrace you,
Where the presence of God will ever leave you.

Contents

How to Know the Will of God

Introduction

Isidor Isaac Rabi was a Nobel Prize winner in Physics and one of the team that produced the atomic bomb. He was once asked how he became a scientist. He replied that every day after school his mother would talk to him about his day. She wasn't so much interested in what he had learned, but how he conducted himself in his studies. She always inquired, "Did you ask a good question today?" "Asking good questions," he said, "made me become a scientist."

The greatest question you can ever ask is, "What is the will of God for my life?" The answer to this affects everything about you forever.

So let me say at the start of this book that the only way you will ever truly and fully discover the answer to that question will be found in Jesus Christ. Therefore I will be sharing with you a great deal about Him as you read through these pages because you cannot discover God's will without Him. Jesus is not only the path to life but He is also the only way through life if you are to live it as God intends.

The greatest peace, contentment and joy we can ever know will always be in the centre of God's will. I will never forget the impact a missionary to communist Russia made on me when I was a new Christian. He said he was often asked if he was ever afraid travelling and ministering behind the Iron Curtain. He admitted there were such times but added, "I am safer in the centre of Moscow in the will of God than I am driving down a motorway in Britain out of it."

When we become followers of Jesus the desire to do His will becomes a part of our new nature. As we develop our relationship with Him His will for us becomes a natural course that leads us into His plans and purposes.

When Jesus was preparing His disciples for His departure, He told them, *"I no longer call you servants, for a servant does not know what His master does. But I have called you friends, for everything that I have heard from my father I have made known to you,"* John 15:15.

Elisabeth Elliot, wife of the famous missionary martyr Jim Elliot, shares these deeply comforting words about discovering the will of God,

> It is evident that the anxiety that shadowed too many days was that I should miss the path of righteousness...but the years since have proved me over and over again that the heart set to do the Father's will need never fear defeat. His promises of guidance may be fully counted upon. Does it make sense to believe that the Shepherd would care less about getting His sheep where He wants them to go than they care about getting there?

When our heart is surrendered to God we are in His will and He will lead us. We do not have to live in the fear of missing it but we can live in the joy of knowing and doing it.

I know the plans I have for you.

Jeremiah 29:11

1

God Has a Plan

"Who am I?"

"Why am I here?"

"What am I here for?"

"Where am I going?"

These are the big questions of life and even though you can exist and never discover the answers you only begin to live when you do.

Singers, philosophers, playwrights, actors, comedians have all asked the questions and given their observations on life.

> *"Does anybody know what we're living for?"* asked Freddie Mercury, the lead singer of the rock group *Queen.*

> *"Life's but a walking shadow, a poor player that struts and frets his hour upon the stage and then is heard no more,"* observes Shakespeare's Macbeth.

> *"There are two tragedies in life. One is not to get your heart's desire. The other is to get it,"* wrote Bernard Shaw, Irish writer and lecturer.

The famous French painter Paul Gauguin was first a sailor, then a stockbroker but in 1885 he left his wife and five children to take up life as an artist. He spent much time overseas before spending his final years in poverty, disease and despair in Tahiti. So deep was his despair that in 1897 Gauguin attempted suicide. He failed and lived for another five years. It was during this time in Tahiti that he painted what is considered one of his greatest masterpieces, a three paneled work entitled *"Where do we come from? What are we? Where are we going?"* The first panel shows three women and a child, representing the beginning of life; *"Where do we come from?"* The middle panel shows the daily existence of young adults – *"What are we?"* The third panel shows an old woman approaching death – *"Where are we going?"*

The three questions are written in small print in the bottom corner of the painting and Gauguin, tormented by his fears and despair, died longing to find the answers.

Bernard Levin was one of Britain's most famous newspaper columnists. He once wrote an article called *Life's Great Riddle, and No Time to Find its Meaning.* He said that in spite of his great success as a newspaper columnist for over twenty years he feared that he might have "wasted reality in the chase of a dream." He wrote,

> "To put it bluntly, have I tried to discover why I was born before I die? I have not managed to answer the question yet, and however many years I have before me they are certainly not as many as there are behind. There is an obvious danger in leaving it too late...why do I have to know why I was born? Because, of course, I am unable to believe that it was an accident; and if it wasn't one, it must have a meaning."

Leo Tolstoy was one of Russia's and the world's greatest writers who wrote such classics as *War and Peace* and *Anna Karenina*. But a few years after such works had made him famous he wrote another book in 1879 called *A Confession* or *My Confession* in which he tells the story of his search for meaning and purpose in life. He had rejected Christianity as a child and when he left university he sought to get as much pleasure out of life as he could. He entered the social world of Moscow and St Petersburg, drinking heavily, living promiscuously, gambling and leading a wild life. But these could not satisfy him.

He had also inherited an estate and made a large amount of money from his books, writing what *Encyclopedia Britannica* describes as "one of the two or three greatest novels in world literature". Fame, success and importance came but no lasting satisfaction or purpose. He said he was surrounded by what appeared to be complete happiness and yet one question brought him to the verge of suicide, "Is there any meaning in my life which will not be annihilated by the inevitability of death that awaits me?"

Tolstoy tells us he eventually found what he was looking for among the peasant people of Russia and their Christian faith. He came to realize that only in Jesus Christ do we find the answer. In his book *Anna Karenina* he refers to the great Christian revival that came to St Petersburg which had a great affect upon both the 'peasants' and aristocracy. Social and cultural traditions were challenged and confronted as these two groups would eat and fellowship together putting aside their social standing.

Not long ago my wife Jan and I were driving from Wales to Scotland for several weeks ministry. The journey is beautiful but long. If you keep the radio on you can hear the hourly news at least ten times. It was a Saturday evening and we were listening to BBC Radio 2 and the presenter of the programme, Clive Anderson, was interviewing Mick Hucknall (lead singer of the group *Simply Red*) about his latest album. Anderson said that he had enjoyed listening to the songs but they seemed "like a cry for help to a catchy tune." Then he added to which Hucknall agreed, "I suppose all popular music could be described that way – a cry for help to catchy tunes."

It was a fascinating insight and what made it even more poignant was that previously on the radio there had been intense news coverage and discussion concerning the tragic death of Charles Kennedy. He had been a very popular Member of Parliament who had served his constituency in the West of Scotland faithfully for many years and was a former leader of the Liberal Democratic Party, but had just lost his Parliamentary seat in the General Election. He was found dead in his home after days of heavy drinking. He had battled alcoholism for years.

There was a huge outpouring of grief and sadness by those who spoke highly of him as a Parliamentarian and a politician. There were also lots of questions asked and discussions as to what made someone with still so much to live for 'self-destruct' with alcohol in such a way. The debate then widened as to why there are so many other intelligent, gifted and educated people (our nation has never been so well educated) who are destroying their life, health, family and future by all kinds of harmful actions and addictions.

Part of the answer is that even though we have never had so much to live with many in our secular society have also never had so little to live for. Possessions without purpose can become highly destructive.

One commentator discussing Charles Kennedy's heavy drinking quipped that people in the Scottish Highlands don't go to psychiatrists with their problems – they have whisky instead.

Our world is filled with fear and pain. Someone observed that babies are usually born into it crying to prepare them for what's to come, and they had never seen or heard of a baby born laughing.

As we journey through life there are two primary experiences most people look for and long for at an emotional level. They are what drive us no matter what our level of education or sophistication. We can even pride and deceive ourselves that we live out of our reason and intelligence but when it comes down to it, where the tyre hits the road, what most of us are led and driven by are;

i)   *How do we maximize our pleasure?*

ii)   *How do we medicate our pain?*

This is what drives so many and is behind every passion and addiction both good and bad. The alcoholic starts with the pleasure and the buzz the drink gives them and then finds in it comfort and relief when life is stressful and they are hurting. It helps to manage the stress but can end up controlling them and even though they know it's destroying them they seem powerless against it. The same is true with every destructive addiction and passion whether it is sex and pornography, money and possessions or it could be food and work that is out of control.

This is why it is so important for us that the source of our delight and our comfort is found in God. If we do not maximize our pleasure and medicate our pain in Him then we will look for it wherever we can.

Jeremiah 29

The year 597 BC was not a good one in Israel's history. The prophet Jeremiah had been warning the nation for years that unless the people changed their ways judgement would come. He had paid a heavy price for speaking the truth and the many false prophets in the land railed against him prophesying everything was alright spiritually and socially with the people. But Jeremiah was proved right and the Babylonians invaded the land and destroyed everything. The city of Jerusalem was laid waste, the Temple was laid to ruins and all its treasures carried off to Babylon. It is from this time that the Ark of the Covenant that symbolised God's presence goes missing. It was either hidden by the Jewish priests or taken away as a trophy of conquest. The inhabitants of Judah were mostly killed or taken captive into exile to Babylon which was one of the most pagan cities on the earth.

The Psalmist captures the pain and despair of the Israelites at this time as he describes how the people mourned,

> *By the rivers of Babylon we sat and wept when we remembered Zion. There on the poplars we hung our harps, for there our captors asked us for songs, our tormentors demanded songs of joy; they said, "Sing us one of the songs of Zion!" How can we sing the songs of the LORD while in a foreign land?*

> Psalm 137:1-4

Into the midst of their pain and the consequences of their own rebellion, God speaks to the nation and says,

> *"For I know the plans I have for you," declares the LORD, "plans to prosper you and not to harm you, plans to give you hope and a future."*

Jeremiah 29:11

Whenever you read in the Bible God referred to as **LORD** (JEHOVAH) in all capitals it refers to Him in His covenant relationship with His people. In contrast when it is spelt **Lord,** with letters lower case, it generally refers to His creator rulership over all creation.

God is reminding the nation that though they have lost Jerusalem and the Temple, they have not lost Him. He is still their God and they are still His people. They may have lost the Ark of the Covenant but He is still their God of the Covenant.

He says that He has not forgotten them and they are always on His mind. He promises to protect and keep them even in Babylon. He tells them to increase and prosper and pray for the place they are in and the people they are with. His purpose is to bless them and to make them a blessing wherever they are.

Note, He doesn't say, "I know the plans I had for you," but rather, *"the plans I still have for you."* He is saying He is still thinking of them and has not forgotten them.

This morning when you woke up God was thinking about you and right now as you read these words whatever you are going through you are on His mind and in His heart. When a friend says, "I have been thinking about you and praying for you" it encourages and empowers us because it helps us to know how much we are loved and cared about.

A Hope and a Future

"Hope" means "a strong and confident expectation." It is connected to trust and faith in God. This is why the devil is constantly attacking our hope because he knows that *"faith is the substance of things hoped for,"* Hebrews 11:1. When our hope is gone our faith gets lost. One of my favourite descriptions of it is that "hope is hearing the music of the future while faith is dancing to it today." But if you don't hear the music it's difficult to keep in time and step with the dance. We must let our hopes and not our hurts shape our future.

When Dr Roger Bannister ran the world's first four-minute mile on May 6, 1954, he did what many believed was physically impossible. *Forbes* magazine declared, after interviewing a number of sports experts, that Roger Bannister's three minute 59.4 second mile was "the greatest athletic achievement" of all time.

For many years it was widely believed to be impossible for a human being to run a mile in under four minutes. It was thought to be a physical barrier no athlete could break without causing significant damage to their health. It had also become a major psychological barrier. Many athletes came close but try as they might no one was able to run a sub four-minute mile. It was as elusive as the pot of gold at the end of the rainbow, spoken of and dreamt about but unachievable.

When Bannister broke four minutes he released the power of hope in others that it could be done. Six weeks after his superhuman achievement the Australian athlete John Landy, who had once said it was impossible, ran the mile in three minutes 58 seconds, breaking Bannister's record. During the next three years, another sixteen runners also broke the four-minute mile.

A while ago my wife and I celebrated over 34 years of marriage. I sometimes tell her that spending forever with her will not be long enough. It makes her smile and helps me if I have done something to annoy her. We have actually known each other for over 51 years as we were in junior school together. In fact for much of the next eleven years of school life we were in the same class. Strange as it seems however, during all that time neither of us can remember saying a single word to each other. I sometimes jokingly say we never had an argument because we never spoke.

About two years after leaving school I found myself attending the same church as Jan and now I really began to like her and wanted to ask her out, but I was apprehensive and worried she would say no. What changed things was one day at church she gave me a smile and that gave me hope. Then we became friendly and hope began to rise until finally faith started to flow and I asked her out on a date. She flung her arms around me and jumped for joy – not quite, but she said yes and from that initial flicker of hope began a beautiful relationship.

There was another reason why God spoke to the exiles in Babylon about their future; it was to remind them of their present. He tells them to settle for a time in Babylon and to only marry among themselves and increase in number, but the long-term plan is that one day their children will return home to Jerusalem. While in that foreign country they were never to forget their identity and destiny. They were to be a part of it for a time but it was never to become a part of them.

God allowed them to be exiled there to change and refine them. Some of them became great leaders that influenced the whole Babylonian Empire, men like Daniel, Shadrach, Meshach and Abednego. People who kept their integrity and brought God's presence and purpose into a pagan nation.

He also promised to give them a future because a person without a future will always be controlled by their past. One of the most destructive things you can ever believe is that you do not have a future. In God's kingdom, whatever age we are the best is always still to come which means that our future will always be greater than our past.

Some years ago, my wife and I had the opportunity to visit the spectacular waterfalls at Niagara. They are immensely impressive with more than three thousand tons of water every second cascading over them creating a spectacular atmosphere of sight and sound. One painting captured it with such intensity that you could almost feel the rush and the power of the water. The problem was that the artist couldn't think of a suitable title for it when the work was displayed in an art gallery. After much thought and discussion they called it, *More to Follow*. Every second there was another three thousand two hundred tons of water cascading majestically over the Falls.

It is the same with God's love and power as it can never be diminished or depleted because it flows out of who He is.

When Jeremiah walked through the burnt-out ruins of Jerusalem he wept with the tears of a man saying, "I told you so," but also with the compassion that was crying out, "God still loves you so." In the midst of his lamentations hope rose within him,

Yet this I call to mind and therefore I have hope: Because of the LORD'S great love we are not consumed, for his compassions never fail. They are new every morning; great is your faithfulness.

Lamentations 3:23-25

Seventy years later after a series of supernatural and amazing events the exiles started to return to Jerusalem from Babylon exactly as God had promised.

How to Know the Will of God

The will of God is not something
you add to your life, it is
a course you choose.

Elisabeth Elliot

How to Know the Will of God

2

Your Life Has a Purpose

Mark Twain, the American author, once said, "The two most important days in a person's life are the day they were born and the day they find out why." Sadly, many people never find out the reason why because until we connect with the God who made us we will never know what He created us for.

Let me rephrase Mark Twain's comment and say that the three most important days in a person's life are, first when they are born, second when they are born again and the third when they discover what they were born again for.

Your life has a God given purpose. You are not an accident or a mistake. Neither are you unimportant or insignificant. You have eternal value and God loves you so much He made you in His likeness. That image, however, has become distorted and disfigured because of sin which means humanity is by nature terribly complex and conflicted, capable of both beautiful and hideous acts. There is within us all the heart of a rebel but also that of a worshipper. A fierce self-rule wants to make us the "master of our own soul," for, *"We all like sheep have gone astray, each of us to our **own** way,"* Isaiah 53:4. We want to be in charge of our own decisions and destiny and in the words of the popular song be able to say, *"I did it my way."* Yet there is also a part of us that is always looking for something or someone to worship. We move from selfishness to servitude, from an antagonism to adoration, from independence to idolatry.

Consider the words of Gerald May, a psychiatrist and a Christian,

> We all have secrets in our hearts... All my life I have longed to say, 'yes', to give myself completely to some Ultimate Someone... I kept this secret for many years because it did not fit the image I wanted to present – that of an independent self-sufficient man. This desire to surrender myself had been at least partially acceptable when I was a child, but as a man I tried to put away childish things. When I became a physician and later a psychiatrist it was still more difficult for me to admit – even to myself – that something in me was searching for ultimate surrender. Society had taught me to say 'no' rather than 'yes', to try to determine my own destiny rather than give myself, to seek mastery rather than surrender.

There is also within us a desire to live for the now as if nothing else matters but at the same time we search for something greater that will last longer because God has set eternity within our hearts.

Sadly, many people never discover or have lost their purpose in life and are just filling in the time. As one wit said, "They are already dead but they have not made it official yet." They are like the epitaph that read, "Died age thirty. Buried aged seventy." One of the great paradoxes of our day is that so many people are both bored and busy at the same time. This is because being bored does not always mean having nothing to do but rather you question the value and the purpose of the things you are so busy doing. Sociologists and psychologists are now telling us that boredom is one of the greatest problems people have.

How to Discover Your God Given Purpose

There was once a fisherman who caught a beautiful fish; it was the first salmon he had ever managed to catch. As he reeled it in he could not help but notice the liquid beauty and gracefulness with which it moved in the water. It was a joy to behold. He lifted it out of the water in his net and laid it on the grass bank of the river. After several moments of wriggling and flapping the fish just lay there with its eyes staring vacantly into the blue sky. It was now immobile and looked rather pitiful. The grass was luscious and soft but the fish just stared benignly. It didn't appreciate its new surroundings or the pictures its captor was taking and it just looked immensely sad like a 'fish out of water!' Soon it would die.

Then the angler put his hands underneath it and gently carried it back to the river. A few moments in the crystal clear waters and the fish began moving again and then suddenly off it swam like liquid ballet. Powerful, graceful, effortless and joyful because this is where it belonged and where all its gifts and graces found their meaning and purpose.

To help discover our purpose and what we were made for and "why on earth we are here!" we need to ask ourselves three very important questions:

i).   *What am I passionate about?*

What is it that I love doing and lights my fire?

29

Passion helps us to connect with purpose; it is a great empowerer. What we love doing we find the energy and time for, but we have to be careful because it's possible to be passionate about something we are not really good at. One of the worst solos I have ever heard in church was a lady who loved singing and thought she could sing but sadly it was painful to everyone who heard her. Now I know God looks at the heart but the problem was we had to listen to the voice. If you have ever watched *Britain's Got Talent* or other such 'talent shows,' you will know exactly what I mean. Some of the most passionate people who audition are sadly some of the most talentless. We laugh and cringe at the same time watching and listening to them. When I see and hear them I wonder at two things; first where is their sense? And secondly where are all their friends to tell them the truth?

ii).   What am I good at?

None of us are good at everything but all of us can be good at something. Our purpose is usually connected to what we are able to do well. At this point we need to be careful of two dangerous extremes, arrogant pride and false humility.

Pride has been described as being like bad breath. Everyone else knows you've got it but you are the last to find out. In the spiritual realm pride is the armour of darkness. But false humility can also destroy your God given purpose by either holding you back or being just a more subtle form of pride and foolishness.

One of the funniest stories I heard explaining this was about a young talented cricket player who had just scored a century and returned to the rest of his team mates who were congratulating him profusely. As a new Christian he wasn't sure how to take all the applause for the talent God had given him and boldly announced to his fellow players, "Oh, it wasn't me." They looked at him shocked and exclaimed, "Then who was it?"

True humility is not thinking you are nothing but realising that Jesus is everything and that in Him you are someone special. It's saying, "I don't care who gets the credit as long as God gets the glory." I love the story of the new minister at his first church who preached really well but didn't know how to take a compliment. After the service one of the older members came to encourage him and said he had given a great sermon. The young preacher replied, "It wasn't me it was God." The old timer smiled and put his arm around him and said, "Young man, it wasn't that good."

iii). What do I do that God is Blessing?

In the world the first two questions are usually enough but in the Kingdom, there is this third question which is the most important one of all. You may be a good communicator and public speaker but it's God's blessing that turns this into ministry and ministering to others. You may have a great voice but there is a huge difference between singing a solo and ministering in song or preaching a sermon and ministering the Word.

When you are passionate about something and are good at it and God is also blessing it then you are flowing in God's purpose for your life.

So the challenge is to know why God created and saved us. When we do this life becomes meaningful and full of purpose. We become more secure and stable and even though we are pilgrims in this world we do not wander aimlessly through life. We become focused and know how to set goals and what dreams to dream. We understand the big picture and don't let not understanding all the small details confuse and frustrate us. We learn to live out of God's promises not needing explanations for everything. Once we find ourselves we are then in a position to lose ourselves for something that is much bigger and greater than we are. Jesus spoke about this when He said,

> *If anyone would come after me, he must deny himself and take up his cross and follow me. For whoever wants to save his life will lose it, but whoever loses his life for me and for the gospel will save it. What good is it for a man to gain the whole world, yet forfeit his soul? Or what can a man give in exchange for his soul?*
>
> Mark 8:24-37

We may become famous or we may not. We may become wealthy or we may not. We may win awards or we may not. All these things are incidental, what matters most is that we take hold of that for which God has taken hold of us.

Charles Colson was a chief aide to the former US President Richard Nixon. He was sent to jail in 1974 for crimes he committed surrounding the Watergate scandal that also saw Nixon removed from office.

A friend of Colson's, Tom Phillips, witnessed to him about the love of God. Colson described years later how when he got back into his car afterward he was shaken and just sat there and cried for an hour. He said,

> God heard my cry. From the next morning I never looked back. I can honestly say that the worst day of

the last 35 years has been better than the best days of the 41 that preceded it. That's a pretty bold statement, given my time in prison, three major surgeries, and two kids with cancer at the same time, but it is absolutely true.

That's because, for the last 35 years – whether in pain, suffering, joy or jubilation, it makes no difference – I have known there was a purpose. I have known that I belong to Christ and that I am here on earth to advance His kingdom.

Colson's time in prison was not wasted. There God planted the seeds in his heart that became a ministry that would impact the world. Colson established *Prison Fellowship International,* which today is active in 120 countries and is the largest association of national Christian ministries working within the criminal justice field.

In recognition of his work, he received the prestigious *Templeton Prize for Progress in Religion* (1993). *The Presidential Citizens Medal* (2008). The *Others Award* from the Salvation Army (1990), and several honorary doctorates. He also wrote more than thirty books which have sold over five million copies.

He went home to be with his Lord in 2012, still faithfully working within prison ministry and justice reform to the end of his days. He then received the greatest award of all when Jesus said to him, *"Well done good and faithful servant...,* enter into the joy of your Lord,"* Matthew 25:23.

Choose life, not death.

Deuteronomy 30:19

3

Choose Life, Not Death

There was once a man whose lucky number was five and he resided at number 555 on Fifth Street. He lived on the fifth floor and his apartment had five rooms. He was married and had five children. One day he saw a horse called Lucky Five who was running in the fifth race at 5.55pm. So he took out all his savings and put £5,000 on the horse. And sure enough the horse came in fifth.

Poor choices, however well intentioned, invariably end up in heartache and suffering. While not all choices affect life at the same level, nevertheless every choice has an affect upon our life and others.

Dr R. T. Kendal, the Christian author and former minister of Westminster Chapel in London, writes, "There is a popular saying that goes, 'There but for the grace of God go I.' It's not a Bible text but is quite close. The full truth is, 'There but for the grace of God and the choices I made go I.'"

Life is made up of choices and consequences. If you want good outcomes you must make good inputs. A good life consists of good choices and decisions. Even the things in life we do not choose that happen to us, we make the choice as to how we respond to them.

One of reasons life is both easier and yet more stressful today is because of the vast variety of choices that exist. Twenty-five years ago we had a choice of five television channels and would often complain after flicking through them that there was nothing to watch. Today we have five hundred channels and spend forever flicking through them and still say there is nothing to watch.

I used to work in a bakery and in those days there were about a dozen different types of bread, but today you can almost spend your holiday at the supermarket trying to choose the loaf of bread you want out of the hundreds of varieties on offer. There is also a vast array of other choices that our forefathers did not have, such as which career to pursue or university to attend and where to live or even what country to live in. Life is far more complex and can therefore be much more confusing and challenging. So how do we make good choices?

In the book of Proverbs wisdom is referred to around fifty times and the heart is mentioned about seventy times.

Wisdom is supreme; therefore get wisdom.

Proverbs 4:7

I guide you in the way of wisdom and lead you along straight paths.

Proverbs 4:11

Trust in the LORD with all your heart and lean not on your own understanding; in all your ways acknowledge him, and he will make your paths straight.

Proverbs 3:5,6

Knowledge can enable us to make a living but it is wisdom that empowers us to make a life that is worth living. The tragedy today is that we have an explosion of information and knowledge but an emptiness of wisdom and understanding. This creates a society where many have never had so much to live with but so little to live for. It means that we are the most educated and informed generation there has ever been but with an epidemic of emptiness, addiction and bondages. Whenever we are told a new study shows a massive increase in sexually transmitted diseases, the use of pornography among children, the abuse of alcohol with teenagers or the crippling effects of debt among adults, to name but a few, the experts and politicians tell us what we need is more education and information. What they don't tell us is that we have never been so well educated and informed.

This brings us to the heart of the issue which is the issue of the heart, and the Book of Proverbs speaks about this extensively.

The Bible describes the heart as the master control area of a person's life. It defines who we are and what we become. What captures it controls our lives, determines our decisions, our direction and destiny. Your heart can become a treasure or a traitor depending upon what fills it. It can deceive you as it can be deceitful above all things (Jeremiah 17:9) or it can direct you as God's revelation comes to it (Ephesians 1:18).

What determines the choices we make and the direction we take more than anything else will be the passions and priorities and the values and virtues that capture our hearts. This is why Solomon tells us, *"Above all else guard your heart for from it come the issues of life,"* Proverbs 4:23.

Knowing and even more importantly doing the will of God is not about trying to follow rules but having a relationship with Him. When we *"acknowledge (know) Him in all our ways He will direct our paths."* This word 'acknowledge' means to be in close relationship. Discovering God's will is not a formula from Him but a fellowship with Him.

The reason why there are times God doesn't show us His will straight away is because He wants to draw us closer to Him before He discloses what He wants us to do. It's because in His presence and knowing Him we find the strength and desire to do what He reveals to us. It's also there we learn to trust Him and that His ways are always best even when we don't understand why.

One of the greatest privileges and freedoms God gave to us is the freedom to choose. When He created mankind He wanted relationship not robotics. He made us to love and be loved which has to involve the power of choice.

When Moses gave final instructions to the Israelites before they entered into the Promised Land he commanded them to make the right choices, however God still gave them the freedom to choose.

> *This day I call heaven and earth as witnesses against you that I have set before you life and death, blessings and curses. Now choose life, so that you and your children may live and that you may love the LORD your God, listen to his voice, and hold fast to him. For the LORD is your life.*
>
> Deuteronomy 30:19,20

There is a story told about an old man in an African village who was reported to be the wisest person in the country. Everyone went to him for advice and marvelled at his wisdom. This brought him great admiration but also a lot of envy. One young man challenged him to a test to determine who was the most knowledgeable. He went to him holding a butterfly in his hands and asked the old man to say whether or not the creature was dead or alive. If he said alive the young man would crush it to show he was wrong but if he said dead, then he would open his hands and let it fly away. The crowd waited for the response and the wise man replied looking into the eyes of the young man, "Life or death, it's in your own hands, you must decide."

The greatest choice we can ever make is what we decide about Jesus. We have all made bad choices at times but they don't have to be the end of the story because Jesus died for our bad choices. He offers us what every human being needs – forgiveness.

He chose to die to give His life for us and then rise again from the grave to give His life to us, but to receive His forgiveness we must be willing to give Him our life.

How to Know the Will of God

Where God's finger points
His hand will make a way.

4

Thy Kingdom Come,
Thy Will Be Done

What is God's will in every situation? Let me tell you because Jesus has already told us, it is that His Kingdom comes on earth as it is in heaven. In seeking to know the will of God this is the place to start.

Yet while prayer is one of our greatest comforts it can also be very confusing. Our prayers get answered and sometimes they don't, at least not the way we want them to or expect. Someone prays for a promotion at work and then is made redundant. They ask God to heal someone and the person gets worse. We pray for direction and find ourselves in the wrong place at the worst time. Yet other times our prayers get answered in exactly the way we want them to.

I don't claim to know all the reasons why this happens. There is the reality and the mystery of prayer that we have to hold in tension until God reveals the answers. Billy Graham's late wife, Ruth, once said, "I thank God for all the prayers He has answered for me and especially the ones He didn't. If He had said yes to all of them I would have married the wrong man, twice."

One of the reasons we become confused is because we do not start with the main purpose of God's will which is the coming of His kingdom on the earth. Therefore, the more we know

45

about His nature and His kingdom the more we will understand His will.

"Our Father" – Knowing the God of the Will

To know the will of God we need to know the God who's will we desire. In the world's most famous prayer He is described as both a Father and a King. Therefore, when we come to Him it is either as a child to a father, as a sinner to a saviour or as a subject to a king. This connection between His relationship with us and rulership over us is the basis for everything else mentioned in what we call *The Lord's Prayer.*

The good news is that He is the most forgiving King and loving Father you will ever know. He is a ruler who comes to us in Christ and is willing to wash feet, embrace lepers and die on a cross. He is also a Father who will never forsake us and promises to meet our every need.

As a King He makes laws for our welfare and as our Father He helps us to keep them and can also lovingly restore us if we break them.

Jesus told a parable about a wayward son which the writer Charles Dickens called the greatest short story ever written. It reveals the darkness of the human condition and the depths of God's love.

The key to understanding the story we refer to as *The Prodigal Son* is knowing about the people Jesus was telling it to at the time.

> *Now the tax collectors and sinners were all gathering around him to hear him. But the*

Pharisees and the teachers of the Law muttered,
'This man welcomes sinners and eats with them.'

Luke 15:1,2

The Pharisees and teachers of the Law believed God rejected and punished sinners. It was only people like themselves who kept the Law whom God welcomed and rewarded. The *'tax collectors and sinners'* were considered the lowest of the low who had no regard for God's laws and commands.

Jesus tells this amazing story to show them there is no one so bad or far from God that they cannot be restored and forgiven, and there are none who think themselves so righteous they don't need to repent and receive forgiveness.

There are these two groups of people, the religious and the rebellious, and Jesus says both need to be forgiven and restored. The prodigal is a type of the sinners and tax collectors lost in the far country while the elder brother is a picture of the Pharisees and teachers of the Law equally lost at home. It's a sobering thought that not only can you be in the world away from God but also in a church and be equally far from Him.

The Father Ran

When the wayward son finally came to his senses and returned home Jesus said that his father saw him from a long way off. This means he was watching and waiting for him and when he saw his son he ran to meet him. This is one of only two occasions in the Bible where God is referred to as running. The other is in the Song of Songs 1:4 where it says, *"Draw me unto you and let us run together."*

47

It was Aristotle, the Greek philosopher, who said that it was the mark of a great man in ancient societies that he did not run. Such haste was considered unseemly by anyone who had standing in society. In the first century a Middle Eastern man of any importance never ran. If he were to run, he would have to pull up his tunic so as not to trip. Doing this would also expose his bare legs which in the culture of the day was considered humiliating and shaming.

Kenneth Bailey, author of *The Cross and the Prodigal,* explains in his book that if a Jewish son lost his inheritance among gentiles and then returned home, the community would perform a ceremony called the *Kezazah.* They would break a large pot in front of him and shout, "You are now cut off from your people." The town or village would totally reject him for what he had done and the shame and disrespect he had brought on his family and community.

So why did the father run? It was because he loved his son and wanted to be the first to welcome him. This way the prodigal would not suffer the rejection of the community. This is also shown by the command to bring a robe, shoes and ring which were all signs of acceptance and restoration.

Jesus says this is what our heavenly Father is like, when we take one step to Him He runs toward us.

The father falls on the returning prodigal's neck and kisses him, the Greek language conveys that he kept kissing him, and that he fully restored him.

His Kingdom Come

Everything about God's Kingdom is positive and full of life. It is love, joy, peace, blessing, health, strength, grace, mercy and everything that is good because it reflects the king who rules over it. Whereas everything about the devil's kingdom is negative and full of death. It is darkness, misery, pain, disease, despair, bondage, cursing, suffering and everything that is bad because it reveals the nature of the one who rules it.

The scriptures make it clear that we live in the tension of God's Kingdom having already come but the fullness of it is still yet to arrive. This means that God heals and promises health, but there are also times when we become sick and are not healed and until Jesus returns and fully establishes the Kingdom we still die.

This is also why Jesus spoke of both the mystery and the reality of the Kingdom at work in our world. Nevertheless, it provides us with the place to begin when wanting to know and do God's will because His will in every life and situation is that His Kingdom rule and purpose comes.

The more we know God's nature and understand His Kingdom the better we are able to know His will for our lives. He will never lead us contrary to His character or His purposes. This is why Jesus says that we are to *"seek first the Kingdom of God and His righteousness and everything else will be given to us,"* Matthew 6:33.

God's will for us is always righteous and He will only lead us in *"paths of righteousness,"* Psalm 23:3. The right way will always be a righteous way.

Rule and Reign

The nation in which I live is called the United Kingdom. It is also called Great Britain and the British Isles. The three titles actually refer to different aspects of my country. The United Kingdom refers to the political union between England, Wales, Scotland and Northern Ireland. Whereas Great Britain is the collective name for England, Scotland and Wales and their associated islands but does not include Northern Ireland. While the British Isles is purely a geographical term referring to the islands of Great Britain and Ireland, including the Republic of Ireland and the five thousand islands scattered around the coasts.

I often tell people there are two other important things you need to know about the United Kingdom. The first is that we are not always as united as we should be. Besides the divisions between the Welsh, Irish, Scots and English there are also divisive distinctions between the north and south of each country. This is often revealed in sporting rivalries and the jokes we tell about each other. One of my favourites is about two Welshmen, two Irishmen, two Scots and two Englishmen all left in a room together as a social study to see what would happen. After about ten minutes the two Welshmen got together and started to sing, while the Scotsmen began a Highland dance and the two Irishmen started to fight. Two hours later the two Englishmen were still waiting to be introduced. Our cultures as well as our countries can be quite different.

More importantly the United Kingdom is not a "kingdom" in the true sense of the word and especially in the Biblical understanding of Kingdom. It is a country with a constitutional monarchy which means that the monarch reigns but they don't rule. Our Queen, who is loved and respected, has reigned for over sixty-four years but it is Parliament that rules by the democratic vote of the people. She has great influence and authority but it is all overseen by Parliament.

On its state opening each year the monarch reads the speech that sets out the Government's agenda for the coming session but it is written by the Prime Minister and the Government. The King or Queen can only read what they have been given.

The Kingdom of God is not like this as it is an "absolute monarchy" where the king not only reigns but rules. He does not have to consult a government or take a vote. There is no higher power or authority. His will is law but because of what He is like it is also love. He is a ruler who passionately wants what is best for His people. He is a king who was willing to give His life for them. A king willing to wash feet even of those who would disappoint and betray Him.

To fully enjoy the blessings of this Kingdom, however, its people need to be willing to be good subjects. This means that they not only desire His *reign* but also His *rule.* When seeking to know God's will both aspects are important.

The problem we can have is that we want the reign without submitting to the rule. We can want God to reign over our finances but not allow Him to rule within our pockets. We can desire His reign over our health but don't want Him to rule in what we do with our bodies. We look for His direction in reigning over our destiny but fail to allow Him to rule in the decisions we make.

In his book *Seeking the Face of God,* the best-selling author Gary Thomas says that, "Christian health is not defined by how happy we are, how prosperous or healthy we are, or even by how many people we have led to the Lord in the past year. Christian health is ultimately defined by how sincerely we wave our flag of surrender."

If you truly want to know the will of God for your life then you must learn to surrender to His reign and His rule. The Bible calls it making Him Lord and it is the most wonderful and liberating choice you will ever make.

Begin each day by saying,

"Loving Heavenly Father, Holy is your Name. Your Kingdom reign and rule come in my life today and help me to live with you and for you. My greatest desire is to know you more and do your will. Amen."

The Sovereign LORD *has given me an instructed tongue, to know the word that sustains the weary. He wakens me morning by morning, wakens my ear to listen like one being taught.*

Isaiah 50:4

5

Hearing the Voice of God

One of my spiritual heroes is a man called C.T. Studd who lived and ministered over a hundred years ago. He was one of the finest cricketers of his day. On one occasion he persuaded several of his England cricket teammates to go and hear the famous American Evangelist D.L. Moody preach with some of them responding to his gospel message. Studd's passion for Jesus took him to China, India and finally Africa turning his back on a life of fame and fortune as he came from a wealthy family background. He founded a society called WEC (*World Evangelism Crusade*) which is still active today.

At the height of his fame as a young man there came a time of crisis about what he should do with his life. During this period his brother George was seriously ill and thought to be dying. C.T. was constantly at his bedside and whilst sitting there watching and waiting as he hovered between life and death these thoughts came welling up in his mind, "Now what is all the popularity of the world worth to George?" (George was also a famous cricketer). "What is all the fame and flattery worth? What is it worth to possess all the riches in the world when a man comes to face eternity?" His brother was restored to health but C.T. was never the same.

He now wanted to know what his life's work should be. He later wrote, "I wanted only to serve God and prayed that He would show me." Then began a very confusing time as even Christian friends and family tried to dissuade him from his heart's desire to go on the mission field. So he went and spent three months in Bible reading and prayer seeking God's direction. He believed God was leading him to go as a missionary to China. One night a close Christian friend came to stay and tried to change Studd's mind. His immediate response was to say, "Let's not argue but right now pray for the Lord's guidance. I don't want to be pig headed I just want to do His will." He later wrote, "That night I could not sleep but it seemed as though I heard someone say these words over and over *'Ask of me and I will give thee the heathen for your inheritance and the uttermost parts of the world for thy possession.'* I knew it was God's voice speaking to me and that I must go to China." Go he did and he became a world changer.

When D.L. Moody was once asked, "How do you know the voice of God?" He replied, "If I went into a room of two hundred women and walked around I would hear the voice of my mother above the rest, not because she had a stronger voice, but because of our relationship my ear has been tuned to it."

Hearing God's voice is relational not mechanical. Jesus said, *"My sheep hear my voice,"* John 10:27. The issue isn't whether or not God speaks but are we in a place to hear and understand what He is saying?

In the early days of the communications industry an advert was placed for a position to take up an important post within a government department that handled sensitive information.

Those who reached a final shortlist were asked to meet in a hotel lobby where they prepared for their interview by the personnel manager. While this final group waited they attempted to assess their chances by comparing their credentials and experiences. The usual background music was playing as they talked together.

After only a few minutes the group noticed that one of their number was missing. The assumption was that, having seen the competition he was up against, he had left early in an endeavour to spare himself the embarrassment of rejection. At that moment the personnel manager appeared to tell them that the successful applicant had got the job and that the interviews were now over. Amid cries of astonishment and consternation the remaining group were informed that while they were engrossed in conversation with one another a Morse code message was tapped out over the music asking the applicants to make their way to the interview room. Only one person had done so because his ear was tuned to what the others did not notice. The problem is that we are often so busy listening to our own voice and those of others that we become distracted and fail to hear when God is speaking.

It's said that US President Franklin Roosevelt once got so tired of smiling and saying the usual things to those he greeted at White House receptions he tried a little experiment to find out whether anyone was paying attention to anything he said. As each person came up to him with extended hand, he flashed a big smile and said, "I murdered my grandmother this morning." People overwhelmed with meeting the President in such a grand setting would automatically respond with a smile and comments such as "how lovely" or "just keep up your great work." Everyone heard but nobody seemed to be listening to what he was saying except one foreign diplomat. When the President said, "I murdered my grandmother this morning," the diplomat responded softly, "I'm sure she had it coming to her."

Fifteen times the Bible says, *"He that has an ear to hear, let him hear."* Clearly this is not referring to our physical hearing but rather to our spiritual ears. This is an obvious yet important distinction because mostly God speaking comes from within, not without. There are times when people hear God speak with an audible voice. When I ask groups if anyone has ever heard God speak this way usually around five percent have experienced such dramatic moments, but for the great majority God speaks within.

There are no short cuts to developing 'spiritual ears'. If I was to invite you to a conference titled, *"How to get the most out of God by putting the least effort in and in the quickest possible time"* I wonder how many would attend? After all it seems very inviting but can you see what's wrong? The real joy of hearing and receiving from God comes first and foremost from being in His presence and spending time with Him. It is from this that every other blessing comes. His presence is even more wonderful than His "presents".

Fine Tuning to God's Voice

I once had a radio which had two tuning dials. The first was to find the station I wanted and the second was for fine tuning to cut out any interference and be able to hear more clearly. There are many voices with a lot of spiritual static coming at us and we need to know how to fine tune to hear when it is truly God speaking and what He is saying.

He speaks to our spirit because it is there the Holy Spirit dwells and we are able to discern His voice. If it was always and only an audible physical voice there would be a danger that we could be misled by all the counterfeit voices around us.

When God speaks to our spirit it is not as a third person ("the Lord would say unto you") but as a first person so we experience it as; I feel, I believe, I sense, I hear. His will comes primarily as revelation to our spirit then it is passed as information to our mind to be evaluated and acted upon. This is why the *"renewing of our mind"* is so important in discerning the will and voice of God, Romans 12:1,2.

The main forms in which messages come from the human spirit to the mind are through,

i).   Conscience

Conscience is not the voice of God nor is it infallible but it is a function of our human spirit that is able to apprehend general moral truth and apply it to specific instances in our behaviour, Romans 2:15.

ii).   Intuition

A more down to earth description is 'our gut reaction' or instinct, which is our immediate perception and insight that comes to us directly without analysing or assimilating the situation. It can come as indefinable promptings and feelings or creative insight. It's important to realise we are not talking here about the voice of the Holy Spirit but purely the way in which the human spirit functions. Some people are far more intuitive than others and many women are more so than men which means they can be more sensitive to the spiritual realm in connecting with what is both good or bad.

iii).   The Voice of God

To hear and discern the voice of God our spirit has to be reset and our mind renewed.

Resetting our spirit begins when we are born again and God's Spirit comes and connects and communes with our spirit which came alive to Him in the new birth experience. It was dead before not in the sense that it was inactive but rather cut off from life and fellowship with Him.

The Holy Spirit now dwells in the recreated spirit of the believer. As He illuminates the human spirit, the conscience now begins to deal with the mind and it becomes sensitive to sin and disobedience. Repentance and confession lead to forgiveness and cleansing. As He is obeyed, the Holy Spirit gains authority in the mind opening it to understand the scriptures and know the voice of God. The mind is now enlightened and renewal takes place, however conflicts can also emerge.

The Past

The mind receives inputs from the past as well as the present which come in the form of memories. Some of these we try to recall while others are intrusive and unwelcomed. Past failures, old griefs, unresolved conflicts and broken dreams and betrayals can still traumatize and torment us.

The Flesh

Even after conversion, when the human spirit is born again, there can still be many bondages in the mind as some areas are full of light and open to God while others are still dominated by darkness and so there is a war in the mind. In this condition, although the mind is open to revelation of divine truth and the promptings of the Holy Spirit, it is also open to other things as well. Old thought patterns arise and tempt and surprise us by their persistence and wear us down into a state of defeat and despair.

We discover that areas of the mind are still under the control of old masters. The flesh wars against the spirit and the spirit against the flesh. The battleground becomes the mind and whoever captures this wins the battle for or against temptation.

Understanding this helps us to comprehend our own and others' ability to sometimes get it so amazingly right and at other times horribly wrong. The Apostle Peter is a classic example, one moment he is saying that Jesus is *"the son of the living God"* and being commended, a short time later he is being rebuked as the devil is using his wrong human understanding to hinder God's purposes. Jesus could have said to Peter, "What are you objecting to – my death or my resurrection?" Peter was being controlled by his own human perspective and perceptions.

The Renewal Process

Renewing our mind and being *"renewed in the spirit of our mind,"* is about understanding what's gone wrong and putting it right.

You were taught, with regard to your former way of life, to put off your old self, which is being corrupted by its deceitful desires; to be made new in the attitude of your minds; and to put on the new self, created to be like God in true righteousness and holiness.

Ephesians 4:22-24

We are told to *"put off the old self"*. But how do we do this?

It starts with repentance. The Greek word is *metanoia*, which means a change of direction and a change of mind. It continues as we respond to the Holy Spirit's direction.

We are also to put on the new self and so become more like Jesus. But we cannot jump from the old (stage one) to the new (stage three) without going through stage two the renewing of our mind – which happens through the power of the cross for us and the work of the Holy Spirit within us.

Creating Your Own Light

There is the story of two missionaries walking down a street in Rio de Janeiro discussing the will of God and how they came to be in that country. One said, "I prayed and fasted and God spoke to me clearly from His Word accompanied by a great peace in my heart." The other looked a bit embarrassed as he shared, "I was walking down the high street one day in my home town and looked in a shop window and saw a box of Brazil nuts and thought this must be where I should go." His friend smiled and said, "You should be grateful that you didn't see a Mars bar."

The longing to hear God's voice is a great desire but it can also be the source of great danger. There are so many voices in the natural and spiritual realm that we have to guard ourselves from listening to the wrong ones. We can become so desperate to hear from God that we will receive and believe almost anything.

One of the ways this can happen is the subtle deception by which we seek to create 'our own light' to make happen what we desperately want. It's often seen in church life by the person going to numerous counsellors and only accepting the advice they want to receive and believe. Then they boldly announce how God has spoken to them and confirmed it. They may be sincere but sincerity is not enough, it has to be coupled with humility and truth otherwise you can be proudly and sincerely wrong and deceived. I recall a very tragic case of a young Christian man who came to see me because his confidence in hearing God speak and guide had been totally shattered. He and a friend had travelled to do mission work overseas with only the one way air ticket they could afford. After arriving they quickly ran out of money and became a burden to those they went to help and ended up at the British Embassy pleading for assistance and then being flown back to the UK. They had read amazing stories of how God provided for others and thought it would automatically work for them. What they failed to understand was the spiritual preparation those others had experienced and the deep roots they had in God to hear His voice clearly.

God warns His people through the prophet Isaiah about the danger of seeking to create their own light in discerning the will of God,

Who among you fears the LORD and obeys the word of his servant? Let him who walks in the dark, who has no light, trust in the name of the LORD and rely on his God.

But now, all you who light fires and provide yourselves with flaming torches, go, walk in the light of your fires and of the torches you have set ablaze. This is what you shall receive from my hand: You will lie down in torment.

Isaiah 53:10,11

God is saying that when your way suddenly gets dark, don't be tempted to light your own fire to see the way ahead. Abraham did exactly this when there was no sign of the son and heir that God had promised so he listened to Sarah instead and slept with Hagar. From this union came Ishmael and the Arab nations which have been in conflict with the Jewish people ever since.

God warned the prophet Ezekiel (14:1-4) about those who set up idols in their heart and how He would answer them in accordance with their great idolatry. This happens when we must have that job, relationship, position or possession and we want it until it becomes an idol. The Lord allows us to have it and the consequences that result to bring us back to our senses and to Him.

It reminds me of the story of a very overweight lady whose friends where she worked were trying to help her diet. One day she went into the office with a huge box of fresh cream cakes for her tea break. Her colleagues looked at her with disbelief and asked why all the cakes if she was trying to lose weight? "Well," she replied, "I prayed that if God wanted me to have cream cakes for my tea break there would be a parking space right outside the front door of the cake shop I drive past every day to get here. And sure enough, the twentieth time I drove around the block there was the parking space!" How many times do we drive around something until we find what we want and convince ourselves it is God?

Hearing God Speak

C.T. Studd heard God speak and discerned His ways because He did two very important things, he spent time in His presence and he humbled himself.

* *If you want to hear from God you need to learn to spend time with Him.*

God speaks from His presence.

He spoke to Moses on many occasions and in different ways, from a burning bush and face to face, but always from His presence. Elijah heard clearly from God because he could say, *"The Lord God in whose presence I stand."* God spoke about His Son from a cloud which represented His presence.

The prophet Jeremiah condemned the false prophets who deceived the people, *"God says, They have run with a message I did not give them but if they had stood in my presence they would have spoken my words,"* Jeremiah 23:22.

The closer we come to the Lord the clearer we will hear Him speak and He will say nothing that contradicts what He has already revealed in the Bible.

*   *If you want to hear from God you need to learn to be still and small.*

When Elijah heard the voice of Jezebel's threats he became filled with fear and wanted to die. What restored him was when he came into the presence of God and heard Him speak and it was in a *"still small voice."*

Being still and becoming small can be two of the hardest things for us to do. Stillness and smallness enable us to develop a 'hearing ear' by having a humble and sensitive spirit.

Stillness is not about being quiet but rather our spirit ceasing from busyness and striving. It is not the emptying of the mind but rather the resting and settling of our spirit.

Smallness is about realising how big God is. It is not that we are nothing but rather realizing Jesus is everything. It is not thinking less of ourselves but thinking of ourselves less and focusing on God.

The Difference between Hearing and Listening

There is a difference between hearing and listening just as there is between music and noise or sound and communication. The reason God wants us to seek Him is that we have *"ears to hear what the Spirit is saying."* The religious leaders in Jesus' day heard God speaking but they did not perceive or understand what He said.

Have you ever heard of RAS? It refers to the Reticular Activating System we all have in our brains. It's the part that filters out what is not important to us to be able to focus on what is. This is how it works. If you live by a railway line it will not be long before you hardly hear any trains go by at all. At first the noise may be awful but you learn to filter it out by its familiarity and lack of importance to you. You hear them but the sound doesn't register the same anymore. Yet the same person who sleeps through the noise of a ten thousand ton train hurtling past at 120 mph wakes immediately the new born baby makes the slightest cry or noise in the room next door.

We all have selected listening and it brings our attention to the things we consider most important in our lives. The value we place on hearing God causes us to focus on His voice and cultivate our sensitivity for hearing Him when He speaks.

Next time you take a walk in a forest or a park listen to the sounds around you. Some people hear crickets and grasshoppers, others don't even hear the birds. Or walk down a busy street full of people with noisy vehicles passing by and suddenly drop a few coins on the pavement and watch as people stop and listen. It's amazing how they filter out all the other sounds and hear the money hitting the ground. We hear best what we value most and have taught ourselves to tune into.

Our next door neighbour keeps a parrot in his porch which is across from our front entrance. The bird is very talkative and has developed the ability to almost perfectly imitate my wife's voice saying, "Hello, I'm home," when she comes in our house. On several occasions I have gone to greet her and found it was only the parrot.

The bird also imitates the sound of our door bell and telephone and I have also gone to answer these to find out it was the parrot. However, it doesn't matter how good the parrot's likeness to my wife's voice as it is at best only a copy and at worst a counterfeit. I have quickly learned to tell them apart. The bird has the right sound but that is all. I discern the difference. Also, my wife speaks from her presence which means her communication is not mechanical like the parrot's but is relational. When I hear her voice and she says "I'm home" and I say "That's wonderful, I'll make you a cup of tea," the parrot doesn't have a clue what I am talking about. It is when I am engaged in communion I know who I am talking to and there is relationship and response.

The will of God is love.
And the love of God is not a sentiment in
the divine mind, it is a purpose for the
world. A sovereign and individual
purpose for every individual life.

Elisabeth Elliot

6

The General Will of God

Before we can know God's specific will we need to understand that first and foremost His will for my life is about who I am becoming before what I will be doing.

God's greatest purpose is for us to become more like Jesus and to be transformed into His image (Romans 8:29).

When we understand this we will realise that it is possible for us to be in the right place, at the right time and doing the right things but if we are not becoming more Christ-like we are not in God's will.

The reason why 'becoming' is before 'doing' is because what God desires most is not our activity for Him but our intimacy with Him (this is what Jesus meant when He told Martha that her sister Mary had chosen what was best (Luke 10:42). We may say as Christians that we don't have a religion but a relationship but the problem is we often try and develop this relationship by becoming religious. Our 'doing' has to come out of our 'being' otherwise our identity is defined by what we do for God instead of who we are in Him. If this happens we see our value and worth in terms of our performance and if we fail to achieve we feel failures and worthless.

In becoming like Him we not only discover our identity but also our authority which we need to be able to do His will.

Many times God does not reveal His will because He knows we will not do it or be able to do it – but as we walk with Him, and are transformed by Him, then we will have not only the desire but also the power and authority to do what He tells us.

When someone asks "What is God's will for my life?" they usually mean: "What does He wants me to do?" "Which job should I take?" or "What career path should I follow?" or "Who should I marry?" or "Should I ever marry?" etc. These are all important decisions, but before you come to know God's specific will you need to be living in His general will which has already been revealed. First you need to see the big picture before you come to the fine details.

The great news is that everyone can simply and easily know what God's general will for their life is because it is found in the book He inspired called the Bible, *His word is a lamp to our feet and a light for our path,"* Psalm 119:105.

A rather lonely man went to his local pet shop and wanted an animal to keep him company so the owner recommended buying a parrot who would be able to talk to him as well as keep him company. He bought the most expensive one in the shop but when he took it home the bird didn't speak a word. He returned the parrot to the pet shop and said, "This bird doesn't talk." "Did I sell you a mirror for his cage?" asked the owner. "Parrots love mirrors. They see themselves and can't stop talking." So the man bought a mirror. Next day he returned. The bird still wasn't talking. "How about a ladder?" enquired the store's owner. "Parrots love walking up and down a ladder. A happy parrot is more likely to talk." The man bought a ladder. Sure enough, he was back the next day, the bird still wasn't talking. "Does your parrot have a swing?

If not, that's the problem. He'll relax and talk no end," he was told. The man reluctantly bought a swing and left.

When he walked into the shop the following day the man was more upset than ever. "The parrot died," he said. The pet shop owner was shocked. "I'm so sorry. Tell me, did he ever say a word?" he asked. "Yes, right before he died," he replied. "He said, 'Don't they sell any food at that pet store?'"

We can spend our whole life looking at mirrors, focusing on appearance, climbing ladders, focusing on career success, swinging on swings and living for entertainment and yet in the process starve to death spiritually and emotionally.

Surrendered to God

William Booth, the founder of the Salvation Army, said that the greatness of a person is found in the measure of their surrender to God. What God desires most is us.

Elisabeth Elliot adds, "One does not surrender a life in an instant. That which is lifelong can only be surrendered in a lifetime." In other words surrender is both lifelong and a lifestyle.

Unconditional surrender is not always easy even when it is to a God who loves us so much. It's more than asking Him to tell us what He wants and then being willing to sign up for it. Rather it is signing our name at the bottom of the page and saying "Lord, fill in the details however you want."

The last major recognised revival in England took place in its most easterly town, Lowestoft, in 1921. It's sometimes referred to as the "Forgotten Revival" because many have never heard about it. Yet it impacted not only the town and

East Anglia but had a dramatic effect on the north east fishing ports of Scotland.

One of the key leaders was the Rev Arthur Douglas Brown, a Baptist minister from South London. But it was not before some intense heart searching and struggles that he finally surrendered to God's will for him to become an itinerant evangelist. This is how he describes his journey which he shared at the Keswick Convention in 1922 while speaking on, *"If my people will humble themselves,"* 2 Chronicles 7:14,

> God laid hold of me in the midst of a Sunday evening service, and He nearly broke my heart while I was preaching. I went back to the vestry, locked the door and threw myself down on the hearthrug in front of the vestry fireplace broken hearted. Why? I do not know. My church was filled. I loved my people, and I believe my people loved me. I was as happy there as I could be.

> That night I went home and went straight to my study. My wife told me supper was ready but I could not eat. It was worth having a broken heart for Christ to mend it. I had no supper that night. Christ laid His hand on a proud minister. All November the struggle went on but I would not give way for a work God had been calling me to do. I knew God was right and I was wrong, but I was not prepared to pay the price.

> Then Christmas came and all the joy around me seemed to mock me. He showed me pictures of my congregation and Douglas Brown on his knees in the midst of them. I said, "Lord, you know it is not my work, choose someone else – I will pray for

them. I cannot get into the pulpit and plead with people. It is against my temperament and you made me, it will kill me."

All through January God wrestled with me. There is a 'love that will not let us go'. O how patient God is. It was February 1921, after four months of struggle there came the crisis. I wrote out my resignation to my church, and it was marked with my own tears. I loved the church but felt if I could not be holy I would at least be honest. I felt I could not go on preaching while I had contention with God. That night my resignation lay on my desk. I went to bed but could not sleep.

As I went out of my bedroom door in the early hours of the morning I stumbled over my dog, (a black Labrador). If ever I thanked God for my dog I did that night. As I knelt at my study table, the dog licked my face, he thought I was ill, but as he did that I felt that I did not deserve anybody to love me, I felt an outcast.

Then something happened. I found myself in the loving embrace of Christ for ever and ever and all power and joy and blessedness rolled like a deluge. How did it come I cannot tell you. Perhaps I may when I get to heaven – all explanations are there but the experience is here. That was 2am in the morning. God had waited four months for a man like me. I said, "Lord Jesus, you want me to go into mission work – I love you more than I dislike that."

This was the moment a 'shepherd' was also willing to become a fisherman.

Such surrender requires trust which is the reason why knowing and doing God's will is relational and not 'religional' (I know there's no such word but you know what I mean). We cannot trust someone more than we know them and the better we know them the more we can trust them.

The power of surrender also breaks every negative thing that has a hold upon us. As we are broken bondages are also broken off us.

To be mastered by God is to be free from every other master which is the greatest freedom we can ever know.

The will of God is not something that enslaves us but liberates us. It's as the chorus *Jesus, All To Jesus*, puts it, *"For it's only in Your will that I am free."*

A Caterpillar or a Chameleon

> *Therefore, I urge you, brothers, in view of God's mercy, to offer your bodies as living sacrifices, holy and pleasing to God - this is your spiritual act of worship. Do not conform any longer to the pattern of this world, but be transformed by the renewing of your mind. Then you will be able to test and approve what God's will is - his good, pleasing and perfect will.*
>
> Romans 12:1,2

Caterpillars and chameleons are fascinating creatures for totally opposite reasons. One is able to become transformed from itself and its surroundings while the other is able to conform itself to blend into almost any environment.

The world is constantly applying pressure for us to become captive to its will and the Apostle Paul is saying that if you want to know and do the will of God become a caterpillar and not a chameleon.

It is not just our spiritual souls that God is concerned about but also what we do with our physical bodies. We are told to *"present our bodies"* to God. We can only do this if we are more than just a body.

Paul also says that we must *"renew our mind"*. Again we are only able to do this if we are more than our thoughts. Paul understood that essentially we are 'spirit' and it is from our spirit that we determine what we do with our mind and our body.

It is through doing this that we are able to know what is the *"good, pleasing and perfect will of God."* There seems here to be a progression and a process and that coming into the centre of God's perfect will is often a journey. It's also significant that Paul speaks of *"testing and approving."* This is because we do not so much discover God's will as if it needs to be uncovered but we receive it as we submit and surrender ourselves to Him.

Theologians differentiate between the permissive and perfect will of God. His permissive will is everything He allows to happen in this 'fallen world.' He has given mankind the gift of free choice and allows the consequences of those decisions. This means that not everything that occurs is what God wants but it happens because of our freedom to choose. Whereas His perfect will is not only what He allows but also what He desires and it is this that we should aspire to and what Paul is speaking about.

This Is the Will of God for Your Life

Filled with the Spirit

> *Therefore do not be foolish, but understand what the Lord's will is. Do not get drunk on wine, which leads to debauchery. Instead, be filled with the Spirit.*
>
> Ephesians 5:17,18

Someone once asked the evangelist D.L.Moody why he always told people they needed to keep on being filled with God's Spirit and he answered, "Because we leak." Let me add, it is also because we get drained by the many demands life and people make upon us.

We need to know the person, presence and power of the Holy Spirit continually in our life because we cannot live the life God wants without Him.

There are differing and often conflicting views of what it means in being *"filled with the Spirit,"* especially of how and when this happens. Sadly, we can get so caught up in the controversy and argue about the theory and theology that we miss the reality. When I was baptised (filled) with the Holy Spirit as a young Christian, my prayer was, "Lord, I don't understand all the different arguments or theological positions but I desire everything you have for me and what you want to do in and through me. Fill me with your Holy Spirit." The next day during a church prayer meeting while I was praying in English I also began to pray in a language I had never known before. It was a significant moment in my life where I went from being shy and insecure to having a new passion and boldness for God. It was definitely something that happened to me after I became a Christian but also something I need to know every day in my life.

"Being filled" in Ephesians 5:17 is in what Greek scholars call the present continuous tense. It means to go on being filled and full of the Holy Spirit. It is not a one time occurrence but an ongoing experience. In Acts 2:4 we are told that the disciples and those with them were all *"Filled with the Holy Spirit."* Several weeks later in Acts 4:31 we read that they were all filled again.

Paul uses the analogy of a drunk person. He is illustrating by observation and contrast. Too much wine is destructive and controlling. It affects everything a person says and does. It influences every aspect of someone under its power. Rather we are to be under the affect and control of the Holy Spirit who will influence everything we say and do.

A Thankful Heart

Those who wish to sing always find a song.

Swedish Proverb

Give thanks in all circumstances, for this is God's will for you in Christ Jesus.

1 Thessalonians 5:18

God's will for your life is that you become a thankful person, someone who makes the choice to rejoice and develops a gratitude attitude.

The quality of our lives is related to the quality of our thoughts and the quality of our thoughts is connected to the thankfulness of our hearts to God.

A young child came down from her bedroom one morning saying to her mother, "What a wonderful day." Her surprised mum said, "What do you mean? It's raining torrents outside and the weather forecast is that it will last all week. How can you call such weather wonderful?" "But mother," the little girl replied, "A wonderful day has nothing to do with the weather." It's sad when our joy is at the mercy of whether it rains or not or what other people say or do. It's not what's going on around us but what's happening within us that makes us thankful people.

Scottish minister Alexander Whyte was known for his uplifting prayers in the pulpit. He always found something for which to be grateful. One Sunday morning the weather was so gloomy that one church member thought to himself, "Certainly the preacher won't think of anything for which to thank the Lord on a wretched day like this." Much to his surprise, however, Whyte began by praying, "We thank Thee, O God, that the weather is not always like this."

Thankfulness turns our focus to God and not ourselves or our problems. It is a place of giving but also positions ourselves to receive what God has for us.

C.S.Lewis observed, "We do not really receive something unless we give thanks for it. The very action of saying, 'thank you' and meaning it, opens up the spirit to a true sense of appreciation. In giving thanks something moves inside the centre of our spirits and allows the wonder of what has been done for us to invade us."

On one occasion Jesus healed ten lepers but only one came back to say thank you. Jesus asked where the other nine were, highlighting their ingratitude. The one who returned received a further blessing whereas the others 'missed the moment.'

There are times in our lives when we are blessed but miss the greater moment, thanksgiving makes sure this doesn't happen.

A Sanctified Life

It is God's will that you should be sanctified.

1 Thessalonians 4:3

Sanctified means to be set apart for God.

The only person who can stop you from becoming all God wants you to be and doing all He wants you to do is not the devil or other people or your life circumstances – it is you! We are as holy as we desire and surrendered to be.

The will of God for your life is that you have a passion for purity as *"the pure in heart will see God,"* Matthew 5:8. The word pure here describes someone who loves God with a heart that is undefiled and undivided.

The devil believes that everyone has a price. He even tried to buy Jesus with the kingdoms of the world. Later Jesus could say, *"The prince of this world is coming and he has nothing in me."* The devil is always looking to use the world to gain an entrance into our lives and to do this he tries to ascertain "our price."

With Judas, it was thirty pieces of silver. With Achan, it was a lump of gold and fine clothes. With David, it was the sight of a beautiful woman bathing.

These reminds me of the story of a wealthy man sitting in a café talking with an attractive young lady. In the course of the conversation he pointed to a well-dressed person seated at a corner table. "See that fellow over there? If I offered you a million pound to sleep with him would you do it?" She thought briefly and said, "For a million pounds, yes, I would." A few moments later he pointed to another man standing at the opposite end of the room, "See him over there? If I was to offer you £10 to sleep with him would you?" Her reply was indignant, "Of course not, what kind of person do you think I am?" He replied softly, "You have already told me that, I am just trying to establish your price."

A sanctified life means you are not for sale to fame or fortune or to power and pleasure. The devil and the world cannot buy you because you know you have already been purchased for God by Jesus and belong to Him.

A Good Person

God's will for you is that you be good and do good.

> *For it is God's will that by doing good you should silence the ignorant talk of foolish men.*

> 1 Peter 2:15

The world exalts and is obsessed with greatness but God honours and extols goodness. The highest reward when we go to heaven will be to hear the words from our heavenly Father, *"Well done good and faithful servant."*

The Apostle Peter summed up Jesus' ministry by saying *"He went around doing good,"* Acts:10:38.

You may be considered great in who you are and at what you do but what God is most interested in is – are you good? Are you a good man or a good woman? Are you a good husband or a good wife? Are you a good father or a good mother?

In one of his sermons John Wesley gave this command, "Do all the good you can, in all the ways you can, in all the places you can, at all the times you can, to all the people you can, as long as ever you can."

*God's will is not a puzzle to solve,
it is a person to follow.*

7

The Specific Will of God

When I lived in Scotland I learned to play golf. There are more golf courses there than almost anywhere and it's very affordable. The problem was that even though the courses were beautiful my game wasn't. I would hit a good shot and then a terrible one. My record was losing eleven balls during one round. I was like the golfer with the brand new driver in his bag about to tee off with an old seven iron and a voice from heaven says, "Use the new driver." So the golfer took the big club from his bag and after a few practice swings the voice spoke again, "Use the old seven iron." Anyone who has ever played golf will understand that.

When I finally admitted I needed some help and went for lessons the instructor took me back to basics. There is an old saying that "Practice makes perfect." But that's not entirely true because while good practice may do so bad practice only reinforces what's wrong and can make it worse. I wanted to impress my golf teacher with my shots, however, he wasn't interested in how far I hit the ball but by how I hit it.

My problem, like so many others who try to play golf, was that I could hit some good shots mixed with bad ones and then some really awful ones and the frustrating thing was that

I didn't know why. It wasn't so much hit and miss but hit and hope.

My teacher was far more interested in my swing and my stance than my shots. If I could get these right I would be able to hit good shots regularly whatever the conditions and the course. I wanted an answer to be able to hit the shot but he was far more concerned about teaching me a solution that I could apply any place at any time. This is why solutions are even better than answers and wisdom is better than just knowledge. Whereas knowledge will help you make a living, wisdom will show you how to make a life that is worth living.

A good maths teacher is not only concerned that you get a right answer to the equation because they know it could be a lucky guess or you just copied someone else. They want to know how you come to the answer and will mark you on how you have tried to work it out. The teacher knows once you understand how to solve it you will be able to get every other equation like it right.

Wisdom is knowing the solution. Whatever you face it is wisdom that will give you the strategy, the strategy will bring about the victory and the victory will give God the glory.

What I am about to show you is not just an answer to what is the will of God for your life, but a solution that you will be able to apply at any time and in whatever circumstance you need to make a decision. This is why we read in the book of Proverbs 4:11, *"wisdom will lead us along the right paths."*

The Will of God is not a Tightrope

When we are doing what God has already revealed as His general will we are in a place to know His specific will for our life.

In Acts 16 the Apostle Paul planned to travel into Asia but God would not allow him. Then Paul tried to head towards Bithynia and again the Spirit of God prevented him. One night Paul saw a vision of a man from Macedonia asking for help and he realised that was where he should be going next and the way was made for him. You could say Paul got it wrong twice, but his passion was to do the will of God and when God said "no" he knew that God would make it clear where he should go.

Knowing God's will can be likened to a car's satellite navigation system or GPS. As long as you are travelling in the right direction even if you miss a specific turn or road the system will recalibrate itself to get you to your destination.

The words of Isaiah 30:21 were real in the Apostle Paul's experience,

> *Whether you turn to the right or to the left, your ears will hear a voice behind you, saying, "This is the way; walk in it."*

The Will of God is not a Maze

Mazes can be 'amazing' but they are definitely not what the will of God for your life are like.

God desires to reveal His will even more that we want to know it. It may sometimes seem unclear but it is never meant to be complicated.

Simply love the Lord with all your heart and as you seek Him He will make it clear to you.

Discovering and doing His will is not a puzzle we have to try and solve but a person called Jesus we need to follow. As we walk with Him He will lead us one step at a time.

The Will of God is more like a Dartboard

As we present our lives to God as a *'living sacrifice'* (Romans 12:1) we come onto the dartboard. It's called submission, we submit to God's mission and purpose. He already knows what is best for us, we cannot create it but we can discover it as we seek to live closer to the 'bull's eye' – the centre of what God wants for us.

Getting closer to the "Bull's Eye"

To be in the centre of God's will there are two very important questions we need to ask,

1.   *What will help me to grow the most spiritually?*

2. *What will enable me most to become more like Jesus?*

Let's apply these questions to some real life decisions such as "Should I change my job?" or "Who does God want me to marry?" or "Do I move to another church?" etc.

Many years ago while I was a young minister I was invited to preach at the oldest Pentecostal church in Scotland, in Kilsyth, and spent the afternoon with one of the elders. He told me about a man, Harold Tee, who had been an elder in the church for many years. He worked for the railways at the local station where the railway management kept offering him promotion, however he always turned it down. He said he already had enough to live on financially and promotion would mean less time and energy to fulfil his duties and ministry within the church. When he died his funeral was one of the largest the town had ever seen. He left a legacy that is still touching lives for God. He also wrote many inspired hymns and one of my favourites reflects the life he lived,

> I want my life to be all filled with praise to Thee,
> My precious Lord divine who died for me,
> Let all my will be Thine, controlled by love divine,
> Live out in me Thy life, O Mighty Saviour.
>
> *Thy blessed will divine, with joy I make it mine,*
> *My **heart** shall be Thy throne, and Thine alone.*
> *Choose Thou the path I tread and whither, I am led,*
> *Help me to follow on, O mighty Saviour.*

Harold Tee made the decision not to accept the promotion that was offered and that was right for him as he sought to answer the questions, "Will this help me grow more spiritually?" and "Will it help or hinder what God is calling me to do within the church and His kingdom and become more like Jesus?"

When you are offered a new job or promotion it may be right for you, because your path is different, however, don't accept it automatically. Many families and marriages have been ruined by unwise job and career decisions. They may give you a bigger house but at the same time destroy your home.

What about marriage? For some people it's what God wants while for others it's not, so how do you know if it's right for you and who is Mr or Mrs Right?

Charles Swindoll tells a lovely story about this in his book *Laugh Again.* He talks about those who have learned to live above their circumstances and how they are usually people who possess a well developed sense of humour. He says,

> I met such a person at a conference in Chicago several years ago. We shared a few laughs following a session at which I had spoken. Later she wrote to thank me for adding a little joy to the otherwise ultra serious conference. Her note was a delightfully creative expression of one who had learned to balance the dark side of life with the bright glow of laughter. Among other things she wrote:

> "Humour has done a lot to help me in my spiritual life. How could I have reared twelve children, starting at age 32, and not have had a sense of humour? After your talks last night I was enjoying some relaxed moments with friends I met here. I told them I got married at age 31. I didn't worry about getting married. I left my future in God's hands. But I must tell you, every night I hung a pair of men's trousers on my bed and knelt down to pray this prayer:

Father in heaven, hear my prayer
And grant it if you can;
I've hung a pair of trousers here,
Please fill them with a man."

The following Sunday Swindoll read the letter to his congregation and they enjoyed it immensely. He added, he happened to notice the different reactions of a father and his teenage son. The dad laughed out loud, but the son seemed preoccupied. On that particular Sunday the mother of the family had stayed home with their sick daughter. Obviously neither father nor son mentioned the story, because a couple of weeks later he received a note from the mother:

'Dear Chuck,

I am wondering if I should be worried about something. It has to do with our son. For the last two weeks I have noticed that before our son turns the light out and goes to sleep at night, he hangs a woman's bikini over the foot of his bed... Should I be concerned about this?"

I assured her there was nothing to worry about. And I am pleased to announce that the young man recently married, so maybe the swimsuit idea works.

When it comes to marriage we know immediately that half the population is not the right choice because if you are a man all men are not an option. If you are a woman all women are also not God's will for you. Everyone married to someone else is not God's choice and as a believer those who don't know and love Jesus are also off limits except in exceptional circumstances (these could be when one converts during engagement or a couple who have been living together many years with several children and one has become a Christian and wants to marry the other who has not).

The Bible is our road map for life but God has also given us His Spirit who is our guide. We need both because sometimes we can misread or misinterpret the map or mistakenly hear and understand our guide. The map is what is already revealed in the scripture and our guide is the direction of the Holy Spirit in our life.

Seven Ways God Reveals His Will

1. The Voice of God

God speaks to us through His Word and by His Spirit. He will never say anything that contradicts what He has already revealed but He does reveal more of Himself and His purposes for us.

There have been too many tragic cases of Christians convinced they have 'heard God' and got it horribly wrong. I say this not to bring fear but focus on how we can get it right.

If we are seeking specific direction yet not living in the revealed will of God then we are open to deception and a great deal of pain.

A friend told me about a Christian couple he had met with and he could not believe how much they had deceived themselves. Both of them had left their spouses with whom they had all been members of the same church together. This couple had formed an adulterous relationship but still believed they were doing God's will and that He would greatly use them together. They told my friend that before their meeting with him they had prayed about their situation and God had spoken very clearly to each of them that what they were doing was not wrong and that He was going to bless them. It was incredible self and demonic deception.

2.   *Circumstances, Opportunities and Timing*

Where God's finger points His hand will make a way, so ask yourself; is there a way that God is opening and making clear to me through circumstances and opportunities?

When my wife Jan and I were praying some years ago about her leaving her employment so that she could travel and work with me fulltime, it was a huge decision. As an itinerant ministry my income was not always regular to say the least. I also enjoyed being able to minister and travel in some places where my expenses would not be met because they did not have the resources. I could do this because Jan had a well-paid job that supported us financially. It was 2011 at the height of the financial crisis and we sensed very strongly that the Lord was saying it was time to give up her job and trust Him.

As we prayed about it we became aware the issue wasn't if but when, as we wanted to get the timing right. In January 2012 we thought this would be a good time for Jan to give notice to leave her job but for some reason we did not have a peace that it was the right moment so we left it until the next month. Literally days before she was planning to give her notice to leave an email came from her Human Resource's department saying they were restructuring the company and offering voluntary redundancies. Jan applied and was given the equivalent of a year's wages which we would never have had if she had handed in her notice a few weeks earlier.

Timing is extremely important with the will of God. If we try and make something happen too soon we will not only mess up in the present but also miss what could and should have been for the future.

3. Open and Closed Doors

My wife and I have often prayed when making a major decision "Lord, we are not sure about the direction or timing of this so please make it clear to us by either opening the door fully or closing it completely."

Many years ago we were seriously thinking about moving to a different property and we loved the house and the location. We agreed on a price with the sellers and went to sign at the solicitors but at the last moment had a 'check in our spirit.' Was this the right decision? We did not want to let the seller down after all the agreements we had come to with them but we also didn't want to get it wrong because the financial implications could have been difficult. We sat in the car outside the solicitors and asked God to help us. We told Him we were sorry if we had rushed ahead without seeking Him fully and to show us clearly what we were to do by either opening the door or closing it. Ten minutes later sitting in our solicitor's office we were told that for some reason the sellers had just backed out and had taken the property off the market. Shortly after the housing market suffered a severe price crash.

4. Putting out a Fleece

Gideon did this when God told him to lead an army against the invading Midianites, (Judges 6). It was a huge task for a man who had been in hiding and who did not think too highly

97

of himself. So he asked God to confirm his commission by a wool fleece being left out overnight and remaining dry when the ground around it was wet with dew and then, to make doubly sure the next night the fleece would be wet and the ground around it remain dry. This God did and it encouraged and empowered Gideon to fulfil God's purposes for his life.

We need to be cautious with such things because this was not a pattern or way in which God led His people in the Bible. Even with Gideon the 'fleece' was only another confirmation after God had clearly already revealed to him what He wanted him to do. Answering by the fleece was more of God's allowing rather than His directing.

5.   *Godly and Wise Counsellors*

Pray it through with God and talk it through with spiritually mature people you trust and will tell you the honest truth.

I don't mean that they would lie to you but sometimes people who love us don't want to upset us if they see we have our heart set on something. So share with people who love you enough to say no as well as yes. Sometimes to get God's perspective we need others to help us.

6.   *The Peace of God*

The first thing you lose when you step out of God's will is your peace – if you don't have a peace about it then don't proceed.

Every time you violate the peace rule you will regret it because it is a lot easier to get into situations than to get out of them.

How does this peace operate in our lives when seeking the will of God?

The Umpire who makes the Final Decision

Let the peace of Christ rule in your hearts, since as members of one body you were called to peace.

Colossians 3:15

The word for 'rule' here refers to an umpire or judge who makes the final decision. When peace comes after seeking God it is a positive indicator of the direction we should take.

While there is a great deal of truth in this we also have to be careful in understanding exactly what Paul is saying in the context of the passage because the word 'peace' actually has two distinct meanings. It means both inner harmony with yourself and also outer harmony with those around you. For God's peace to be a guide you must not be living in hostility with your brothers and sisters in Christ.

The Urim and the Thummim: When the Tabernacle was erected, God told the Israelites that specific garments were to be made and worn by the High Priests. These included a breastplate upon which were twelve stones representing the twelve tribes of Israel and the *Urim* (lights) and the *Thummim* (perfections). Scholars are not certain what these were but they may have been precious stones that would shine and indicate God's will.

When the counsel of God was sought the high priest would go into the holy place which was lit only by the lampstand so it was very dim, and he would stand before the veil of the Holy of Holies asking the Lord for guidance. The scriptures say that God would answer by illuminating either the *urim* or *thummim* (Exodus 28:30; Leviticus 8:8; Numbers 27:21; Nehemiah 7:65). The *urim* would indicate a negative response (no) and the *thummim* a positive (yes).

What is significant is that *thummah* (plural of *thummim*) is consistently translated in the Old Testament as integrity or wholeness of heart. This is why we are told in Proverbs 11:3, *"The integrity of the upright guides them."*

When our hearts are right with God His peace will help guide and direct us.

7.   Delight yourself in the Lord

> *Delight yourself in the LORD and he will give you the desires of your heart.*
>
> Psalm 37:4

In seeking God's will we have to get past our own emotions and natural desires. We also have to make sure that other people's expectations and concerns for us do not become a stumbling block.

There was a time in Jesus' ministry when His mother and brothers sought to take charge of Him because they thought He was *"out of His mind,"* Mark 3:21, 31-35. His response was to refuse to see them and declare that, *"Whoever does God's will is my brother, sister and mother."*

In Psalm 37 David shows us how we overcome our own and others desires by God's desire being established in our hearts.

We bring the decision or issue to God and surrender it to Him. Then we 'delight' in Him and thank Him for His goodness and love and that all His ways are righteous and can be trusted.

At this point we don't focus on the choices or desires but on God. This way we bypass our own preferences and submit to His perfect will.

After doing this for a season (days, weeks or maybe months) if the desire in your heart to do something or for someone grows stronger then it is a good indication that God has put it there. If it decreases and dies however, then it is a sign that this is not what God wants.

As we delight in God, He puts His desires into our heart so that they become our desires also. Direction from God comes from delighting in Him.

Let me conclude by saying something about 'prophetic words,' they can bring great clarity but also sometimes cause chaos into a person's life. They may or may not be from the Lord. Sometimes they can also be a mixture of the spiritual and the human.

When they are directive they must always be confirming what God has already said to us or will show us for ourselves. Therefore it is helpful to have them recorded or written down in order to pray them through. We mustn't let them go to our heads but we need to take them to heart and most importantly to God.

Does it make sense to pray for guidance about the future if we are not obeying in the thing that lies before us today?

Elisabeth Elliot

8

Obedience and Perseverance

There was a group of junior executives participating in a management training programme. The seminar leader pounded home his point about the need to make decisions and take action on them. "For instance," he said, "if you had five frogs on a log and three of them decided to jump, how many frogs would you have left on the log?" The answer from the group was unanimous, "Two."

"Wrong," replied the speaker, "there would still be five because there is a big difference between deciding to jump and actually jumping."

I will never forget the time I first prayed out loud in a prayer meeting. I was a young Christian and full of passion and nerves. Finally, after rehearsing the words in my mind for about twenty minutes I felt I would burst if I did not speak them out. The prayer lasted about a minute and I sat down exhausted but so pleased I had finally overcome the sound barrier and hearing my own voice. Almost immediately I sensed God speaking to me and telling me to start singing a chorus. This was an even bigger challenge because I was terrified no one would join in or I would get the words and the key wrong, so I said, "No, Lord."

I now know that, "No, Lord," is a contradiction in terms because if Jesus is Lord the answer to what He wants should be yes. Then the Lord reminded me about what I had just prayed, it was, "Lord, help us to be obedient." I saw the irony straight away and said, "Lord, if you want me to start this chorus I will." And so I began and in doing so got the key completely wrong. I kept going almost alone, my girlfriend (and future wife, Jan) sat next to me trying to suppress her laughter because she and others knew what was coming. I had started the chorus in a key that was far too high and there was coming a line where it would get so high that no human voice would ever reach the notes. When I got there I stopped and prayed out loud for the second time that night, "Lord, maybe I can't sing but at least I am obedient." It was a serious yet funny learning and growing moment. Several people came to me after so encouraged because they had never prayed or spoken out in public and my little endeavour that night had encouraged them, especially the song I got wrong.

Many of you will have come across the beautiful poem called *Footprints in the Sand,* a while ago I came across a different version called *'Butt' Prints in the Sand.*

> One night I had a wondrous dream
> One set of footprints there was seen,
> The footprints of my precious Lord
> But mine were not along the shore.
>
> But then some stranger prints appeared,
> I asked the Lord, "What have we here?"
> "These prints are large and round and neat
> But Lord they are too big for feet."

"My child," he said in sober tones,
"For miles I carried you alone.
I challenged you to walk by faith
But you refused and made me wait.

"You disobeyed, you would not grow,
The walk of faith you would not know.
So I got tired, I got fed up,
And *THERE I DROPPED YOU ON YOUR BUTT.*

"Because in life there comes a time
When one must fight and one must climb,
One must rise and take a stand
Or leave their butt-prints in the sand."

It is one thing to know the will of God but another to do it. Faith may come by hearing but it grows by doing.

Perseverance

> *You need to persevere so that when you have done the will of God, you will receive what he has promised.*

> Hebrews 10:36

Over two hundred years ago one of the most famous sermons ever preached was given by a newly ordained young minister named William Carey. He urged his fellow Baptist leaders at their church conference to become involved in World Missions. His clarion call was for them as a movement to *"Expect great things from God and attempt great things for God."* Mission textbooks agree that Carey's words that day literally changed the world. He became known as The Father of Modern Missions who went and worked in India for over forty years translating the Bible into more than thirty-five languages and dialects. He was appointed to high office by the British Government, founded Serampore College, the first Christian college in Asia and inspired millions to follow his passion to fulfil the Great Commission. He was a very ordinary shoe maker from Northampton, England, who God used to do extraordinary things.

He once explained himself and his achievements to his nephew by saying, "I can plod, that is my only genius, I can persevere in any definite pursuit. To this I owe everything."

There are many who are able to perform but sadly do not have the strength to persevere and so miss the purposes and promises of God.

Perseverance is about our faith and character being developed to be able to receive what God has always desired to give us. Abraham, David and Joseph were promised great things by God yet had to wait many years before they were fulfilled.

Corrie ten Boom and her family were Dutch Christians who helped many Jews escape the Nazi Holocaust of WWII. When their home was raided after an informant tipped off the Nazis of their activities, the entire family was imprisoned. Corrie and her sister were sent to the notorious Nazi concentration camp at Ravensbruck. She was miraculously released from prison just days after her sister had died there. She later travelled the world speaking and ministering to bring God's love and healing to many. She said this about the will of God for her life,

> "There are no 'ifs' in God's Kingdom. His timing is perfect. His will is our hiding place. Lord Jesus, keep me in Your will! Don't let me go mad by poking about outside it."

She would often illustrate what gave her the power to persevere and trust God by showing the two sides of an embroidery. On the one was a mass of knotted silk and cotton but turn it over and on the other side is a beautiful design. She said,

> "Although the threads of my life have often seemed knotted, I know by faith that on the other side of the embroidery is a crown."

She would quote the following poem,

My life is but a weaving
Between my God and me.
I cannot choose the colours
He weaveth steadily.

Oft' times He weaveth sorrow;
And I in foolish pride
Forget He sees the upper
And I the underside.

Not 'til the loom is silent
And the shuttles cease to fly,
Will God unroll the canvas
And reveal the reason why.

The dark threads are as needful
In the weaver's skilful hand,
As the threads of gold and silver
In the pattern He has planned.

He knows, He loves, He cares;
Nothing this truth can dim.
He gives the very best to those
Who leave the choice to Him.

When we are in the will of God we are not told it will be easy but we are promised we will be blessed.

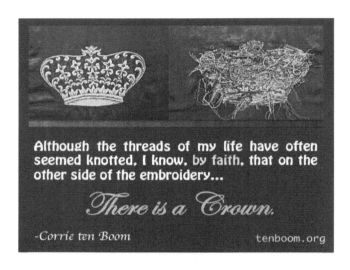

Although the threads of my life have often seemed knotted, I know, by faith, that on the other side of the embroidery...

There is a Crown.

-Corrie ten Boom

tenboom.org

**If you become a settler when God
has called you to move
you will always be a
settler for less.**

How to Know the Will of God

9

When is it Time to Move On?

Seasons change and not everything is forever while some things are only for a short time, so how do we know when it is time to stay, walk or even to run?

There is a parable told about a man who was convinced that God would help him to survive a disastrous impending flood. As the floodwaters began to rise he climbed up onto the roof of his house, when a neighbour came by in a rowing boat he shouted to him to join him in the boat. The man, however, proclaimed, "God will guide me through this! I put all my faith in Him to tell me to either stay or go." The water continued to rise and a few hours later the Coast Guard speedboat came by and the captain informed the man that he must abandon his home and join them on the boat as this might be his last opportunity to be rescued. Again, the man refused and proclaimed, "God will guide me through this! I put all my faith in Him to tell me to either stay or go." Finally, a news helicopter covering the flood noticed the man standing on his roof completely surrounded by water – it would be just minutes before the entire building was covered in water. The helicopter pilot swooped down and tossed a rope to the man and begged him to grab hold or he would surely die. Once again the man proclaimed, "God will guide me through this! I put all my faith in Him to tell me to either stay or go."

The water rose and soon the man did indeed drown. When he stood before St Peter in heaven he confessed his disappointment proclaiming that God had abandoned him in his hour of need. St Peter looked at him and said, "My son, what was it you expected of God? After all, He sent a rowing boat, the Coast Guard and a helicopter to save you, but you turned them all away." Sometimes we can try and be so spiritual that we miss the obvious.

A lady once came to me after I had given a talk about knowing the will of God and described a ministry situation she was working in. She believed God had led her to work in this position however the person in charge of her region had become increasingly controlling and constantly undermined her. So here was her dilemma, she wanted to do the will of God who she believed had led her there but was now unable to do what she felt she was called to do. Should she stay, walk or run?

I said to her the first thing she must do was continue to pray and guard her heart from any offence and resentment. There were spiritual forces at work but also emotional feelings and if she didn't watch against these she would act out of hurt, frustration and confusion. She also needed to try and see what was happening from the other person's perspective and examine her own actions and attitudes in the conflict and tensions that had arisen.

I told her to share with trusted friends for godly counsel and then speak with the person involved and the leaders of the organisation. If nothing changed and she had no peace about staying and there was no prospect of her being able to fulfil the purpose she was called to do then it was a good indication that it was probably time to move on. A few weeks later she spoke with me again and told me that she had done all those things yet her regional leader had made it clear that nothing would change and she now felt the situation was even more controlling and oppressive so she would be moving on. She was willing to continue for a few more months to help the organisation find someone to replace her and would leave on good terms. She seemed so much 'lighter and happier' and was excited about serving God in new opportunities that lay ahead.

So here is the principle: if you believe God called you to a place or position but circumstances or people make it no longer possible to do what God has called you to do and there is little or no prospect of things changing, then maybe it is time to move on. This is only a helpful principle, you need to seek God as He can change impossible circumstances, but we also need to acknowledge that there are times to simply go.

It can often be harder, however, to leave a situation when things are going well than when they are difficult. There are times when our task is done and however much people love us and say all manner of great things about us to keep us, we must be led by the Holy Spirit not by others' desires and persuasion. The believers in Acts 21:12 loved Paul so much they begged him not to go to Jerusalem after a prophet named Agabus had prophesied of the danger and persecution Paul would face if he went there. Paul, however, could not and would not allow himself to be led by all their loving persuasion because he knew God wanted him in Jerusalem. It was the same when Peter said out of great concern that Jesus should not die on a cross, (Matthew 16:22-23) and Jesus had to rebuke him.

To do the will of God we must be careful not to come under the control of people's love, however well meant, or we will be led by sentiment and obligation; neither must we come under a spirit of fear and intimidation. We are not to be pressured to stay or driven away. We must be led by God.

Let God have your life, He can do more with it than you can.

Dwight L. Moody

10

Willing to be made Willing

We have been asking and seeking to answer the question "What is the will of God for our lives?" But what do you do when you know it but don't want to do it or think you are not able to do it?

The answer to this struggle is found in our surrender. We will either submit to the world and our own desires or to the Father and His purposes.

Even Jesus faced this battle in the Garden of Gethsemane as the full horror of the cross began to overwhelm Him. His final response came out of intimacy and surrender to His Father. He said, *"Abba Father... not what I will, but what you will,"* Mark 14:36.

This is the only time the Gospels record Jesus using the term, *"Abba Father."* It means 'daddy' and was the most intimate term a child could express to their father. Jesus is saying, "Daddy, I know how much you love me and I can trust you no matter what lies ahead."

The Power of Surrender

Kathryn Kuhlman was in many ways very ordinary in that she was not a great singer or theologian or even a great preacher but God used her in extraordinary ways. It's reckoned she saw more that a million miracles take place in her meetings and during her ministry. She was a lady who carried the presence of God. She shared a deep insight into this when she said that what God desires most in our lives is not our ability or talents but simply our surrender.

Josef Tson suffered much under the Communist regime in Romania during which he was imprisoned and tortured. Through this the Lord has used him in amazing ways. He said there is a difference between *commitment* and *surrender*. He says, "When you make a commitment, you are still in control no matter how noble the thing you commit to. One can commit to pray, study the Bible, give money or to lose weight. Whatever he or she chooses to do, they commit to it. Surrender is different. If someone holds a gun and asks you to lift your hands in the air as a token of surrender, you don't tell that individual what you are committed to. You simply surrender and do as you are told. The key word is *surrender*. We are to be the slaves of the Lord Jesus Christ."

It is therefore possible to be committed for God without being surrendered to Him. You can be committed to a purpose in His Kingdom yet not totally yielded to the King. Such people are usually characteristised by being more 'driven' than they are 'led.' They become more caught up in His projects than in His person. Their ministry or empire tends to become the focus more than Him and His Kingdom. Surrender is coming to the place when we don't care who gets the credit as long as God gets the glory.

Commitment is knowing what God requires and being willing to do it. While surrender is **not** knowing everything God desires and what it means but still being willing to say "Yes, Lord." Jesus in His humanity would not have known all it meant to be made sin upon the cross but He was willing to surrender His all.

To come to such a place of complete surrender requires four things:

1. Submitting to God
2. Denying the world
3. Focussing on the Kingdom
4. Walking in fellowship with the King

In his wonderful book *Rees Howells Intercessor* Norman Grubb tells the life story of a man who founded the Bible College of Wales. Howells had a profound affect upon the nation and the world. He came from a poor family in a Welsh mining village, but more than anything else he learned the power and secret of prevailing prayer. During World War II Howells and the staff at the Bible College engaged in intercession that had a profound impact on the events of the conflict. The records document amazing answers to their prayers. God had prepared him *'for such a time as this'* but the journey of coming to full surrender to do God's will did not always come easy.

One of the most significant moments came after he attended a Bible week convention at Llandrindrod Wells in Mid Wales in 1906 when he was 26 years of age. He describes an amazing vision he had of the glorified Christ and a powerful encounter with the Holy Spirit where God was calling Him to unconditional surrender. He says the Holy Spirit showed him that every bit of his fallen nature was to go at the cross. It meant that Rees was to give himself completely to God.

Such complete surrender did not come easy to Rees who cried his heart out to God and for the next five days spent the time alone with God. He says, "...the Lord put His finger on each part of my self life and I had to make a decision whether to yield or hold on to it."

As the Holy Spirit began to replace Rees' self-nature with His own nature the first issue He began to deal with was the 'love of money' that had once been such a great motivation in his life. The Lord told him that He would take out of his nature all taste for money and any ambition for the ownership of it. God also dealt with the desire for ambition and reputation.

As Rees battled with his decision and what it would mean the Lord simply asked "Are you willing?" Rees says he was torn, he wanted to say yes but he could not. Then the Lord spoke to him again, "If you can't be willing would you like me to help you? Are you willing to be made willing?" Rees bowed his head and said, "Lord, I am willing to be made willing."

Within an hour the Holy Spirit flooded the whole of Rees Howells' being and he says he was transported to another realm where the Father, the Saviour and the Holy Spirit live. He said, "I have lived there ever since."

The Lord will always enable us to be and to do whatever He asks of us if we are willing to be made willing.

What Will Be Your Legacy?

One morning in 1888 Alfred Nobel opened the newspaper only to find an article about his own death. A careless reporter had confused Alfred with his brother who had indeed died. The shock of reading his own obituary was compounded with the realization of how the world saw him. To the general public he was simply the 'Dynamite King,' a successful industrialist who had amassed a fortune from explosives and the man who had invented dynamite. There was no mention of his ideal of peace for mankind or his efforts for social change and reforms. He would be remembered only for being a 'merchant of death.'

Alfred determined right then that he wanted to do something to make sure the world would recognize the values to which he had devoted his life. He decided that this could be accomplished by the way he disposed of his vast wealth. That's why today we have a prestigious award given annually to individuals or organisations that have contributed significantly to the cause of world peace – the *Nobel Peace Prize.*

What will your legacy be?

It Depends Whose Hands You Are In

A tennis racket in my hands is worth about £30.
A tennis racket in Roger Federer's hands is
Worth about £30 million.
It depends whose hands it's in.

A basketball in my hands is worth about £20.
A basketball in Michael Jordan's hands is worth about £50 million.
It depends whose hands it's in.

A golf club in my hands is not worth very much.
A golf club in Jack Nicklaus' hands is worth about £100 million.
It depends whose hands it's in.

A pen in my hand can write a letter.
A pen in the Apostle Paul's hand can change the world.
It depends whose hands it's in.

A rod in my hands will keep away a wild animal,
A rod in Moses' hands will part the mighty sea.
It depends whose hands it's in.

A sling shot in my hands is a kid's toy.
A sling shot in David's hand is a mighty weapon.
It depends whose hands it's in.

Two fish and five loaves of bread in my hands
is a couple of fish sandwiches.
Two fish and five loaves of bread
in God's hands will feed thousands.
It depends whose hands it's in.

Nails in my hands might produce a dog kennel.
Nails in Jesus Christ's hands will produce
Salvation for the entire world.
It depends whose hands it's in.

So put your concerns, your worries, your fears,
your hopes, your dreams, your families and your
life in God's hands…

Because it all depends whose hands you are in.

Books by David Holdaway

The Life of Jesus
The Life of Jesus More Than A prophet
Never Enough
Money and Spiritual Warfare
Surviving and Succeeding in a Financial Crisis
Was Jesus Rich?
How to Stand Against a Spiritual Attack
No More Fear
Winning Over Worry
The Wonder of Christmas
Jesus The Wonder of Christmas
The Captured Heart
The Burning Heart
Issues of the Heart
Revival is a Heart Issue
They Saw Jesus
Footholds and Strongholds
What Word do all University Professors Spell Wrong?
Insights from the World's Most Famous Song: Psalm 23
How to Know the Will of God for your Life

All these books are available in good book
shops and also by contacting the author.
Teaching and Ministry CDs are also available.
Davidholdaway1@aol.com
www.lifepublications.org.uk
Tel. (+ 44) (0) 1685 371748